JAZZ FLUTE DUETS

MB 98292

BY LENNIE NIEHAUS

AF090320

MEL BAY

Visit us on the Web at www.melbay.com or www.billsmusicshelf.com

Contents

Introduction

Lennie Niehaus is a household word among jazz musicians. Having been a phenomenal jazz saxophonist, he is eminently qualified to write for and understand woodwind instruments. These duets resulted from a conversation we had about the need for jazz flute literature. Most duets were written in the past for saxophone or clarinet. The six duets in this book will be a great addition to the flutist's repertoire.

Sheridon Stokes

Lennie Niehaus

Lennie Niehaus is an award winning composer, arranger and performer whose career has covered a wide spectrum. Born in St. Louis, Lennie graduated Cum Laude from California State University. Joining the Stan Kenton Orchestra in 1952, he toured and recorded on many of Kenton's albums. It was during this time that Downbeat Magazine awarded him the "New Star- Alto Sax" Award. In addition to the albums he composed, and arranged for Kenton, Lennie has nine albums to his credit including his most recent release Live at Capozzoli's on Woofy Records.

While serving in the military, Lennie befriended a fellow soldier – Clint Eastwood. It is through this friendship that he began scoring, arranging and composing for feature films and television. His film scoring credits include Sesame Street Presents: Follow That Bird, City Heat, Tightrope and 13 films for Eastwood (such as Bridges of Madison County, Midnight in the Garden of Good and Evil, Space Cowboys, Unforgiven, and the recently released Blood Work).

Touching on his experiences playing with the masters of bebop in his youth, Lennie composed the award winning score Bird, a tribute to the legendary jazz artist Charlie Parker. He worked closely with actor Forest Whitaker and director Eastwood to capture this essence of the intense and troubled performer. He received a Cannes Film Festi- val Technical Award and a nomination for British Academy Award for his work.
In 1994 he won an Emmy Award for his score to Showtime's film Lush Life and has television credits such as Amazing Stories (the Venessa In the Garden episode), The Child Saver, Titanic, The Jack Bull and Clint Eastwood:Out of the Shadows.

Lennie remains active in music education as a performer, clinician, and adjudicator. He has published numerous works for concert band, orchestra, ensemble, as well as several textbooks on saxophone pedagogy.

Performance Notes

1. Teepee or inverted V is always short
and accented (whether 1/8, 1/4 or tied 1/8s)

2. Tenuto is always full value

3. Any accent is still full note value

4. Unless notated, the accents are not on the beat

5. Everything is legato unless marked otherwise

6. All triplets are to be played evenly

7. Exaggerate the accents and dynamics

8. ***f—p*** means play soft on the repeat

9. Tempo markings are very important

Duet 1

Swing

by Lennie Niehaus
BMI

1. Swing as before
2.
To Coda
25
mf
mf
D.S. al Coda
ff
ff

Duet 2

by Lennie Niehaus
BMI

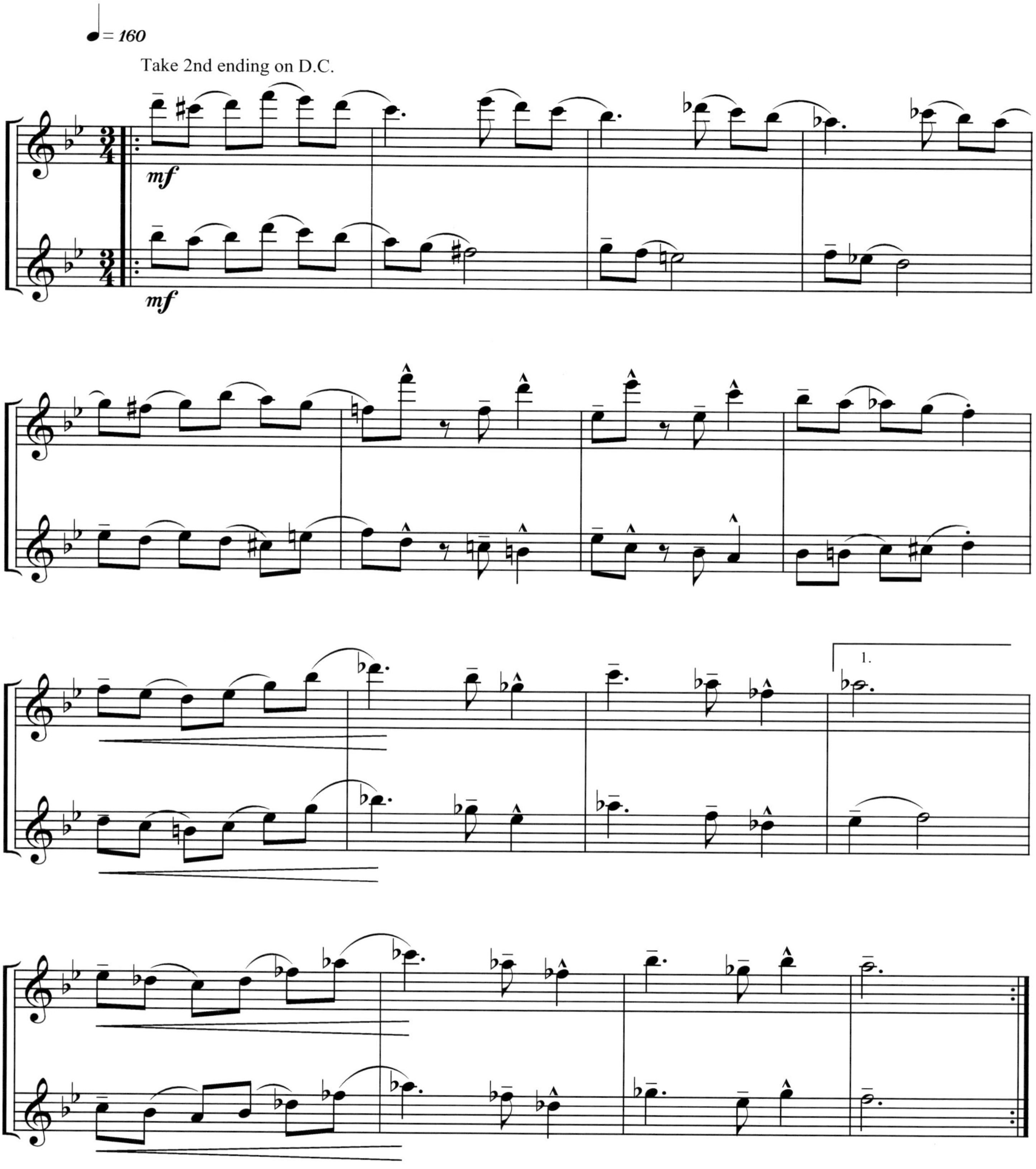

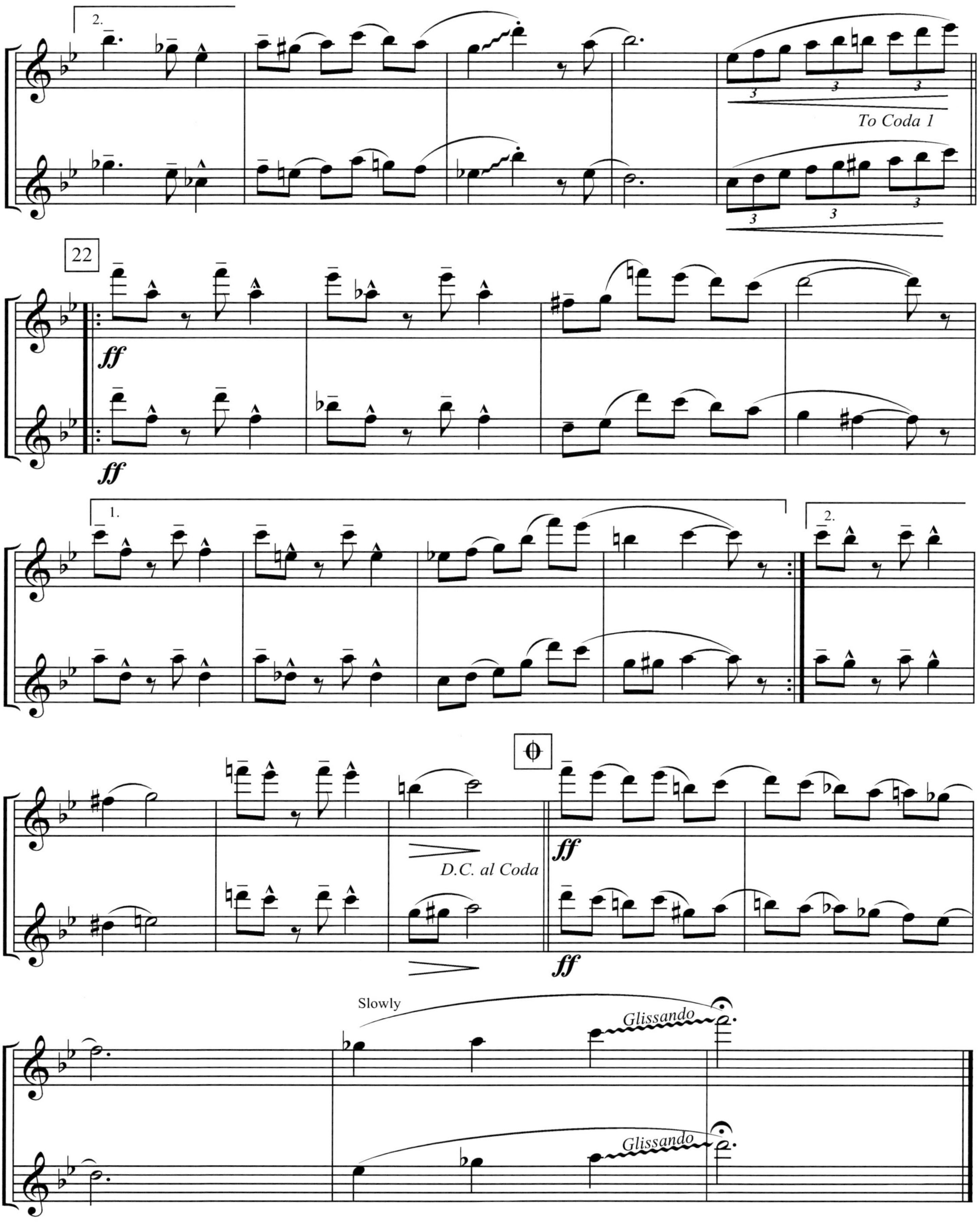
2.
To Coda 1
22
ff
ff
1.
2.
D.C. al Coda
ff
ff
Slowly
Glissando
Glissando

Duet 3

by Lennie Niehaus
BMI

espress.
espress.

Duet 4

by Lennie Niehaus
BMI

2.
3
3
ff
ff
29
fff
f
Fermata
last x only
D.S. al Fine
fff
f
Fermata
last x only

Duet 5

by Lennie Niehaus
BMI

23
fff
fff

Duet 6

by Lennie Niehaus
BMI

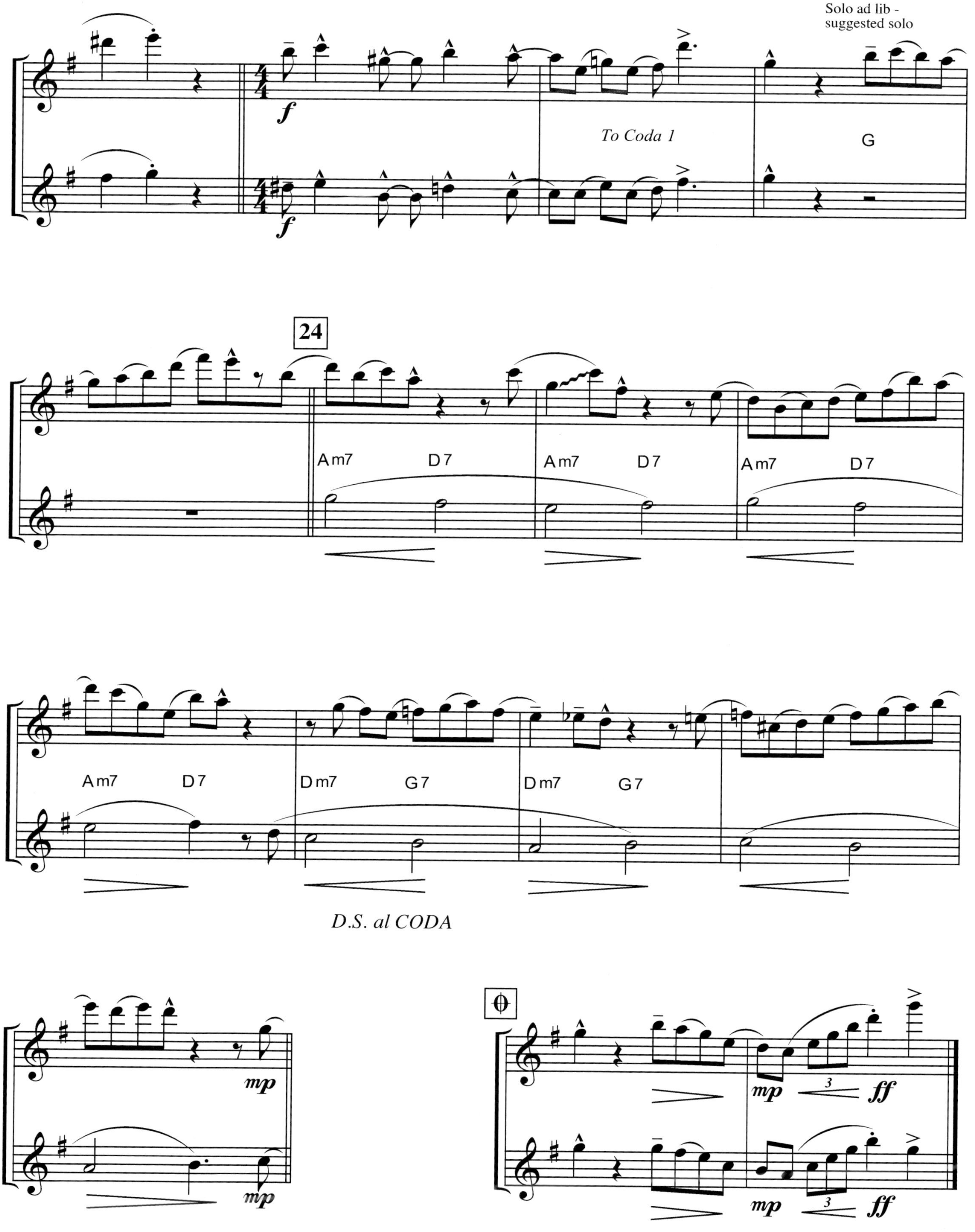
Solo ad lib -
suggested solo
To Coda 1
G
24
Am7 D7
Am7 D7
Am7 D7
Am7 D7
Dm7 G7
Dm7 G7
D.S. al CODA

UNIQUELY INTERESTING MUSIC!

50 GREAT CLASSICS FOR PIANO

ADAGIO SOSTENUTO (*Moonlight Sonata*)	Beethoven	2
CHANSON TRISTE	Tschaikovsky	6
CHANT SANS PAROLES	Tschaikovsky	8
CONSOLATION No 3 in D Flat	Liszt	28
DREAMING (*Träumerei*)	Schumann	12
FUR ELISE	Beethoven	14
GAVOTTE in F	Martini	18
GAVOTTE 1 (*English Suite No 3*)	Bach	22
GAVOTTE 2 (or *Musette*) (*English Suite No 3*)	Bach	23
GOPAK	Moussorgsky	24
THE HARMONIOUS BLACKSMITH	Handel	33
HUNGARIAN DANCE No 5	Brahms	38
HUNGARIAN DANCE No 6	Brahms	42
LARGO	Handel	45
L'AVALANCHE	Heller	48
LE COUCOU	Daquin	50
LIEBESTRÄUME	Liszt	58
LULLABY	Brahms	55
MARCHE FUNÈBRE	Chopin	68
MARCH MILITAIRE	Schubert	64
MELODY	Schumann	158
MELODY in F	Rubinstein	73
THE MERRY PEASANT (*Fröhlicher Landmann*)	Schumann	13
MINUET in A	Boccherini	78
MINUET IN G	Beethoven	82
MOMENTS MUSICAUX No 3	Schubert	84
MOMENTS MUSICAUX No 6	Schubert	86
NOCTURNE No 5 in B Flat	Field	89
NOCTURNE in E Flat	Chopin	94
POLONAISE in A Major	Chopin	98
PRELUDE in C Sharp Minor	Rachmaninoff	104
RONDO ALLA TURCA	Mozart	112
SERENADE	Schubert	108
SERENADE	Haydn	117
SOLDIER'S MARCH	Schumann	159
SOLFEGIETTO	C.P.E. Bach	128
SPRING SONG	Mendelssohn	122
SWEET DREAMS	Tschaikovsky	126
THREE PRELUDES		
PRELUDE in E Minor	Chopin	156
PRELUDE in A Major	Chopin	157
PRELUDE in C Minor	Chopin	157
TOCCATA in A	Paradies	131
FROM MUSICKS HANDMAID		
TRUMPET TUNE	Purcell	136
AIR	Purcell	136
RIGADOON	Purcell	137
VALSE in A Minor	Chopin	138
VALSE in C Sharp Minor	Chopin	144
VENETIAN GONDOLA SONG	Mendelssohn	150
WALTZ in A Minor	Grieg	152
WARUM? (Why?)	Schumann	154

First published in 1985 by International Music Publications Ltd
International Music Publications Ltd is a Faber Music company
Bloomsbury House 74–77 Great Russell Street London WC1B 3DA
Printed in England by Caligraving Ltd

ISBN10: 0-571-53290-X
EAN13: 0-571-53290-2

ADAGIO SOSTENUTO *(Moonlight Sonata)*

Beethoven

dim.
p
cresc.
dim.
p

dim.
pp
come primo
cresc.
p
p

cresc.
cresc.
p
pp
marc.
decresc.
rit.
pp

CHANSON TRISTE

Tschaikovsky

Allegretto non troppo.

la melodia con molto espressione

poco riten.
f
p
mf
pp
morendo
ppp
rit.

CHANT SANS PAROLES

Tschaikovsky

Allegretto grazioso e cantabile.

mf
p
cresc.
f
f
dim.
p poco rit.

a tempo
f
energico
cresc.
ff
p
f

cresc.
ff
p
p
sempre dim.
marcato la melodia
pp
ppp

DREAMING *(Träumerei)*

Schumann

Andante moderato.

THE MERRY PEASANT *(Fröhlicher Landmann)*

Schumann

FUR ELISE

Beethoven

Ped.
C

Ped.
cresc.

p molto leggiero
Ped.

GAVOTTE in F

Martini

ten.
f
Ped.
p
pp dolce
mp
ten.
mf
Ped.

pp
p
ten.
p
f
Ped.
p dolce
f

Ped.
ten.
p dolce
Ped.
cresc.
Ped.
p
cresc.
f
p
f rit.
Ped.
sf

GAVOTTE 1 *English Suite No 3)*

Bach

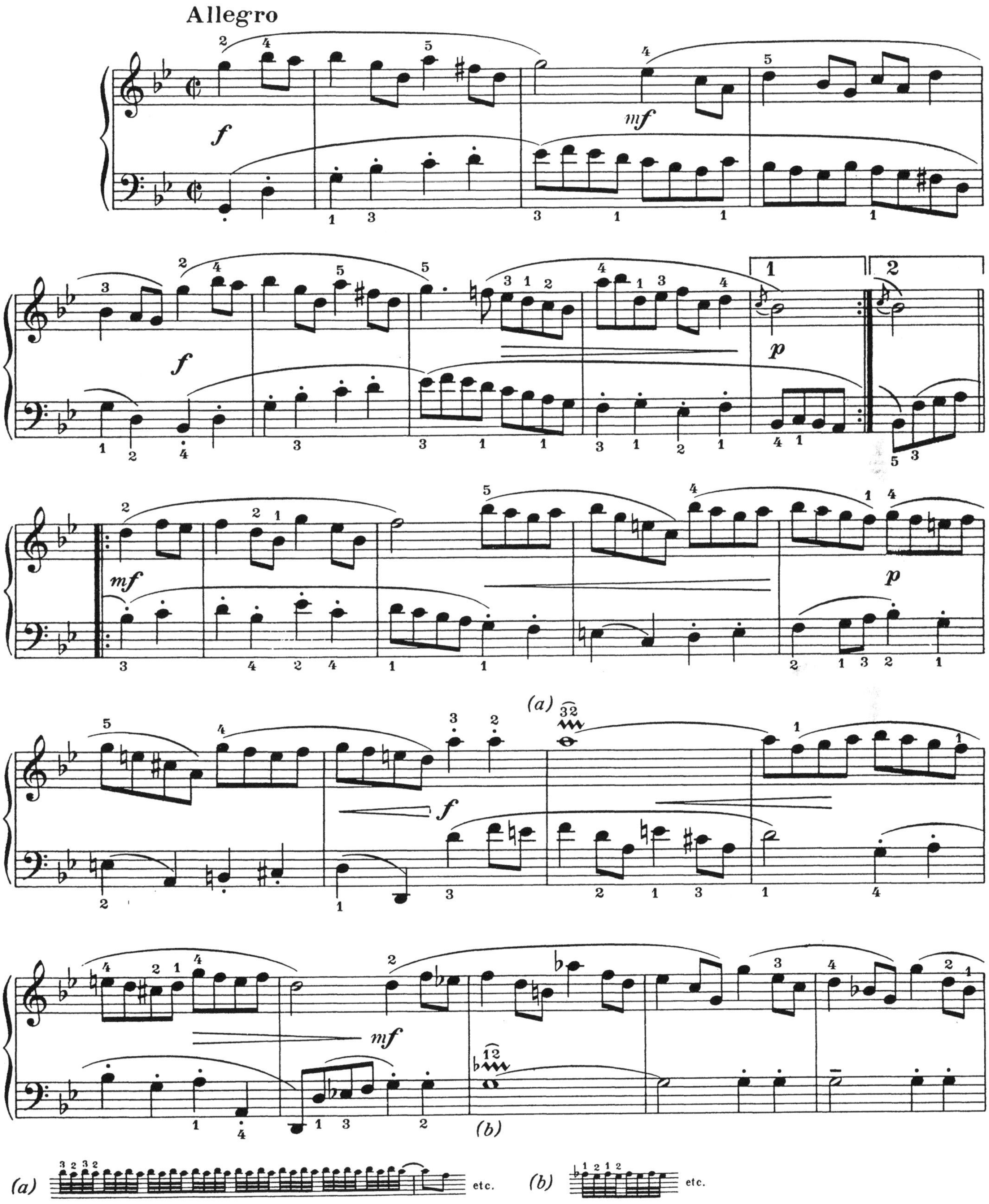

GAVOTTE 2 (or *Mosette*) (*English Suite No 3*)

Bach

GOPAK

Moussorgsky

poco allargando
a tempo
Ped.

f
sf
Ped.
p
poco cresc.
mf
Ped.
sf
Ped.
più cresc. sf
Ped.
sf
Ped.
cresc.
sf
sf
sf
sf
sf
mf
cresc.
Ped.

sf
p
Ped.
f
mf
Ped.
f
Ped.
Ped.
mf
p
pp
8
ppp

CONSOLATION No 3 in D Flat

Liszt

mf espressivo
dolcissimo
mf espressivo

dolcissimo
cresc.
poco rit.
a tempo
l.h.
r.h.
l.h.

smor - zan - - do
ppp
rit. per - den - dosi

THE HARMONIOUS BLACKSMITH

Handel

(a) 

p
(b)
cresc.
VAR. III
leggiero
mf
dim.
mf
p
cresc.
cresc.
f
(b)
or

VAR. IV
mf legg.
f
p
cresc.
tr
VAR. V.
f
p

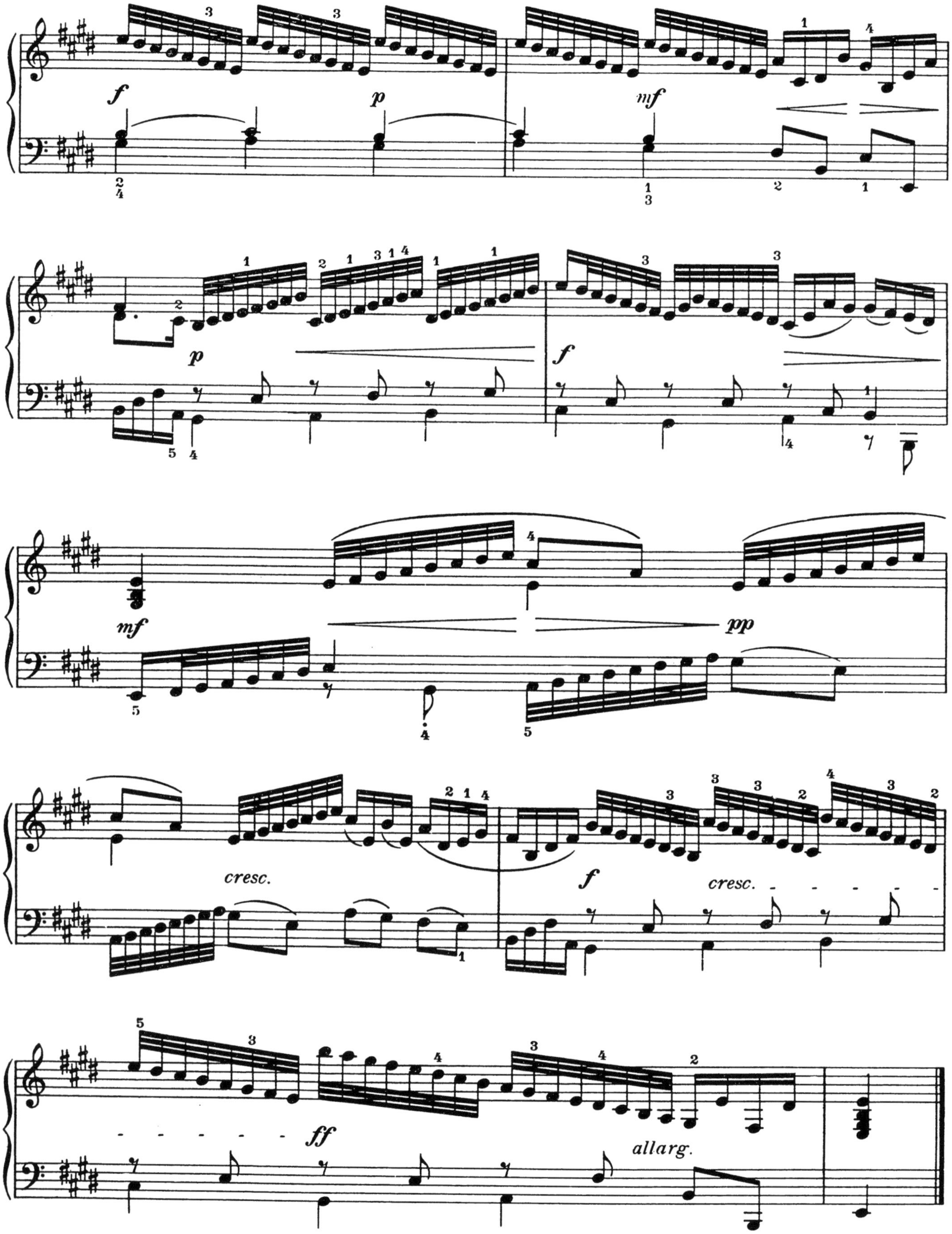
cresc.
cresc.
allarg.

HUNGARIAN DANCE No 5

Brahms

f
p legg.
sf
f marc.
p poco rit.
sf a tempo
f

Vivace
f
sf
f
poco rit.
p
a tempo
poco rit.
a tempo
poco rit.
p
a tempo
poco rit.
a tempo

Tempo I.
passionato
f
8
f
p legg.
8
sf
f marc.
p poco rit.
sf a tempo f
5
f

HUNGARIAN DANCE No 6

Brahms

f molto sostenuto
2nd time loco
p a tempo
vivace
p legg.
1
2
f
sf
p poco sostenuto
più rit.
f vivo
p
f
fz

p sempre vivo
p
f
sf.
mf
p legg.

LARGO

Handel

cresc.

mf
p
f
cresc.
allarg.
ff
a tempo
mf
rall.
p

L'AVALANCHE

Heller

p
Ped.
Ped.
mf
più f
f
più p
Ped.
Ped.
f
risoluto
fp
Ped.
cresc.
8
fz
p
pp

LE COUCOU

Daquin

mf
p
poco dim.
(a)
tr
p

poco cresc.
pp
tr

(a)

p
pp
rit.

LULLABY

Brahms

pp
sempre legato
Ped.
simile
più p

mp
più p
pochiss. rit.
a tempo
senza Ped.
pp
Ped.
calando
rit.

LIEBESTRÄUME

Liszt

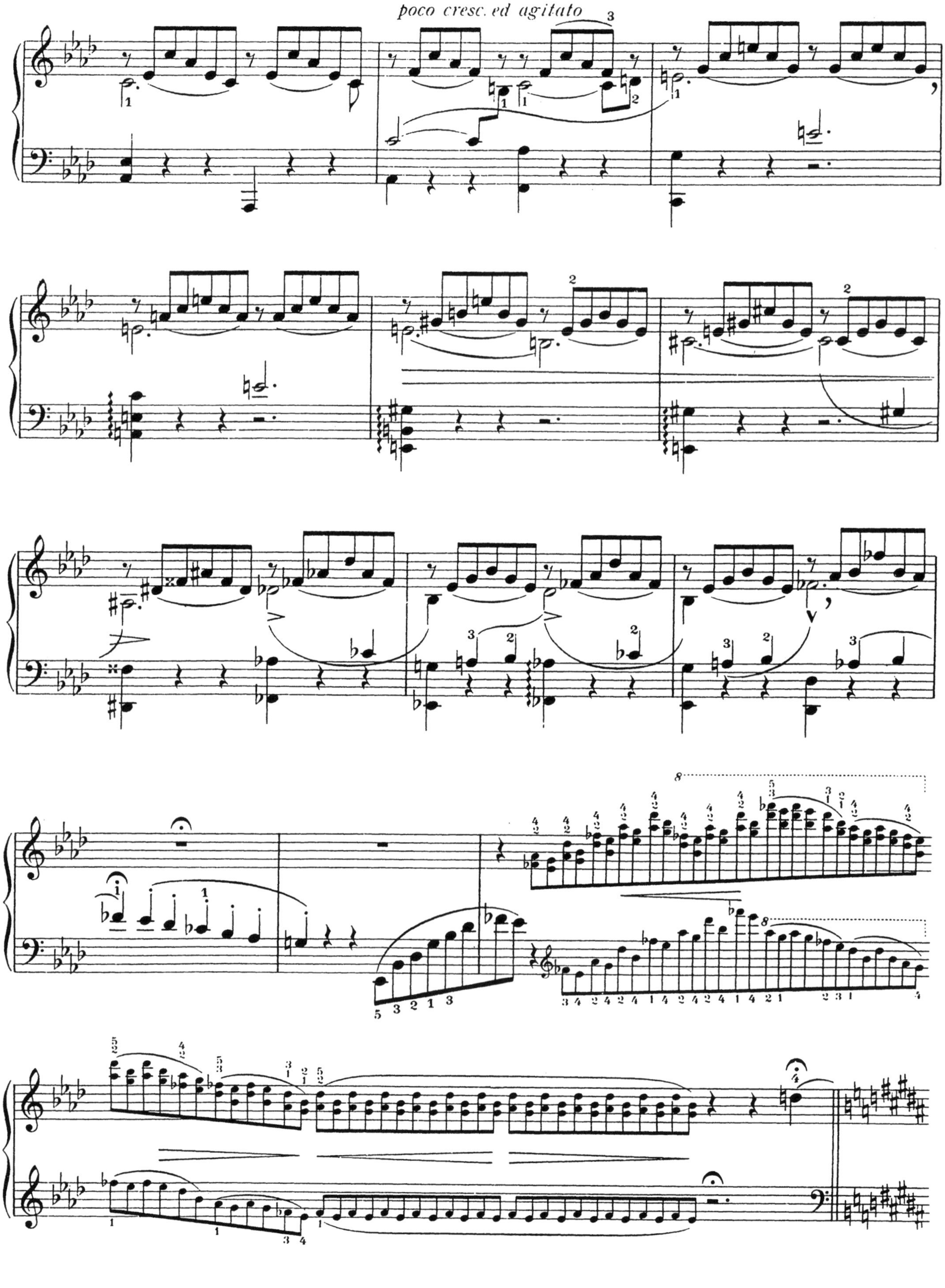
poco cresc. ed agitato

Più animato con passione
sempre crescendo
f
sempre stringendo

ff
sempre più rinforzando
appassionato assai

affrettando
dimin.
leggiero
ritard.
Tempo I.
dolce armonioso
Ped.
Ped.
simile

poco a poco ritenuto
più smorz. e rit.

MARCH MILITAIRE

Schubert

f
mf

Fine.

D.C. al Fine

MARCHE FUNÈBRE

Chopin

sempre f
(a)
sempre f
(a)

cresc.
pp

pp
poco cresc.
cresc.
sf
sf
più cresc.
f

sf
sempre f
tr
p
f
sf
sempre f
tr
p morendo

MELODY in F

Rubinstein

mf
mf
f
rall.
dim.
stringendo
sotto voce
rit.
Tempo I.

p
mf
mf
f
dim.
rall.

stringendo e cresc.
sotto voce
L. H.
rit.
p
Tempo I.
p
f
mf

p
rit.
pp
R. H.
L. H.
8

MINUET in A

Boccherini

(a)

mf
p
rall.
p
a tempo
simile
(a)
rall.
TRIO
p
p
mf
(a)

L.H.
(b)
tr
Ped.
(c)
p
simile

mf
p
rall.
p
a tempo
simile
rall.

MINUET in G

Beethoven

mp
cresc.
dim.
p
mf
p
mf
mf
f
mf
sf
f
sf
sf

MOMENTS MUSICAUX No 3

Schubert

(a) 

pp
pp
p
dim.
p
pp
rall.

MOMENTS MUSICAUX No 6

Schubert

(a) 

pp
cresc.
p
f
p
pp
più p
ff
p
p
pp
Fine

TRIO

Allegretto D. C.

NOCTURNE No 5 in B Flat

Field

mf
dim.
p

p
mp

cresc.
f
mf dim.

8va
f
p
pp
mp
p
p
p
rit.
pp

NOCTURNE in E Flat

Chopin

pp poco rit.
f a tempo
poco rall.
a tempo
fz p
cresc.
p
tr
p
pp poco rit.

f a tempo
poco rall.
a tempo
fz p
cresc.
tr
p
p
pp
poco rubato
pp
dolcissimo

p
con forza
stretto
cresc.
ff senza tempo
p
rall.
pp a tempo
ppp

POLONAISE in A Major

Chopin

ff
f
ff

energico
più f
cresc.
molto cresc.
L.H.

ritenuto
molto cresc.
più f
cresc.
molto cresc.

f
ff
f

ff
f
ff

PRELUDE in C Sharp Minor

Rachmaninoff

Agitato. (♩ = 92.)
mp
cresc.
dim.
mf
cresc.
dim.
cresc.
ff
dim.

accel. molto
cresc.
Presto.
fff
ff
ff
sfff rall.
sfff
Tempo I.
R.H. fff pesante
sfff
L.H. fff pesante
sfff

R.H.
L.H.
sffff
sffff
R.H.
L.H.
dim.
dim.
R.H.
dim.
mf
dim. e poco rall. al Fine.
ppp
L.H.
dim.
mf
ppp

SERENADE

Schubert

p
Ped.
f
mf
pp

p
pp
p
p
f
Ped.

cres.
fp
p dolce.
p
f
f
decres.
perdendosi.
pp
both Pedals.
dim.
Fine.

RONDO ALLA TURCA

Mozart

p
f
p

mf
p
p
cresc.
sf
p
tr
f
1
2
CODA
f
sf
sf

sf
sf
p
ff
fz
fz

SERENADE

Haydn

Andante cantabile

p
cresc.
mf
mf
dim.
mp
cresc.
p
mp
cresc.
p

mf
mp
mf
p
p
mf
dim.
pp

mf
p
mf
p
mf
cresc. poco a poco
f

mp
cresc.
p
mp
cresc.
p
mf
mp
mf
p rall.
pp

SPRING SONG

Mendelssohn

Allegretto grazioso.

rall.
mf
a tempo
f
ten.
p
dolce
dim. e legato
rall.

pp a tempo
Ped.
sf
p
cresc.
mf
a tempo
f

ten.
p
p dolce
p
con grazia
pp
legg.
Ped.

SWEET DREAMS

Tschaikovsky

Andante con molto espressione

mf
f
rit.
p a tempo
poco più f
p
p
f
p rit.
Ped.

SOLFEGIETTO

C.P.E. Bach

(a) *L.H.* above *R.H.*

(a)

TOCCATA in A

Paradies

Allegro (♩ = 116)

p
mf
mf
p
mf

f
p
f
mf
mf

p
mf
p
poco rit.
p a tempo

f
ff
p
f
p
f
cresc. e rit.

FROM MUSICKS HANDMAID

TRUMPET TUNE

Purcell

AIR

Purcell

RIGADOON

Allegro

Purcell

VALSE in A Minor

Chopin

dim.
p
poco più mosso
Ped.
mp
simile
cresc.
sostenuto
f
p

Ped. simile
pp
pochiss rit.
mf a tempo primo
p
cresc.
f
dim.
p

poco più mosso
mp
sostenuto
f
p

pp
pochiss. rit.
a tempo primo
tr
p
tr
poco più mosso
dolce
Ped.
senza Ped.

dim.
Ped.
pp
p
Ped.
pp
Ped.
p
rall.
ten.
a tempo primo
sotto voce
tr
perdendosi
tr
pochiss. rit.

VALSE in C Sharp Minor

Chopin

Più mosso.
legatissimo
Ped.
Ped.
simile
pp

Più lento.
dolce
Ped.
p
rit.

Più mosso.
mf
Ped.
Ped.
simile
pp

Tempo I.
p
Ped.
Ped.
Ped.
Ped.
Ped.
simile
p
p
p
p
mf

Più mosso.
legatissimo
Ped.
Ped.
simile
8
pp
8

VENETIAN GONDOLA SONG

Mendelssohn

f
ff
tr
pp
sf
p
morendo

WALTZ in A Minor

Grieg

Allegro moderato.

p
ritard.
a tempo
ritard.
f
pp
f ritard.
p
Coda.
p dolce
pp
Ped.

WARUM? (Why?)

Schumann

poco rit.

THREE PRELUDES

PRELUDE in E Minor

Chopin

PRELUDE in A Major

Chopin

PRELUDE in C Minor

Chopin

MELODY

Schumann

SOLDIER'S MARCH

Schumann

4/01

Printed in Great Britain by Halstan & Co. Ltd., Amersham, Bucks.